Laurie Krasny Brown, Ed.D., and Marc Brown

WHAT'S THE BIG SECRET?

Talking about Sex with Girls and Boys

LB

LITTLE, BROWN AND COMPANY
New York   Boston

For Dorothy Burlage,
who started us on this project

Special thanks to the following people for their thoughtful and well-informed comments: Dorothy Burlage, clinical psychologist; Morton Herskowitz, psychiatrist; Ann Lombardi, school nurse; Ruth Mayer, SIECUS sex educator; Katherine Morrison, children's library assistant; and Judie Stolp, head of lower school. And thanks to Joan Chapdelaine, head nurse, and Brian Toomey, hospital administrator, for their research assistance for the illustrations.

Little, Brown and Company

Hachette Book Group
1290 Avenue of the Americas, New York, NY 10104
Visit our website at www.lb-kids.com

Little, Brown and Company is a division
of Hachette Book Group, Inc.
The Little, Brown name and logo are trademarks
of Hachette Book Group, Inc.

First Paperback Edition: April 2000

First published in hardcover in September 1997
by Little, Brown and Company

Library of Congress Cataloging-in-Publication Data

Brown, Laurie Krasny.
    What's the big secret? : talking about sex with girls and
boys / Laurie Krasny Brown, Ed.D., and Marc Brown. — 1st ed.
        p.   cm.
    Summary: Answers some of the most common questions about
sex and development.
        ISBN 978-0-316-10915-4 (hc)   ISBN 978-0-316-10183-7 (pb)
        1. Sex instruction for children.   2. Sex differences — Juvenile
literature.   3. Human reproduction — Juvenile literature.   4. Brown,
Marc Tolon.   [1. Sex instruction for children.   2. Sex differences.
3. Reproduction.]   I. Title.
HQ53.B76   1997
6498.65 — dc20   96-15521
                    HC: 10   9   8   7   6   5
                    PB: 20   19   18   17

                            APS
                    Manufactured in China

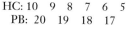

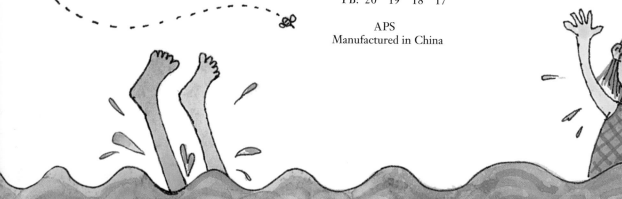

CONTENTS

How Do Boys and Girls Differ?

From the moment your life begins, you are either a boy or a girl. How do you tell boys and girls apart? How do you tell for sure?

Is it their *names?*
Girls and boys do have different names. Sometimes, but not always.

Is it their *clothes?*
Boys and girls do wear different clothes.
Sometimes, but not always.

How about their *hair?*
Girls and boys do have different hairstyles.
Sometimes, but not always.

Maybe the way to tell them apart is by how they *play*. Girls and boys do play in different ways. Sometimes, but not always.

Both girls and boys sometimes like to feel their own strength or be on a team. Other times, they may prefer quiet play.

All sorts of toys, games, and activities appeal to both boys and girls.

Can you tell them apart by the *feelings* they show? Maybe boys are not supposed to get scared, for they might be called a sissy if they do. Maybe girls are not supposed to get mad, for they might be called too wild if they do. Not really!

Both boys and girls have all kinds of feelings.

Knowing your feelings and learning ways to express them is part of growing up.

Bodies
A Little Anatomy Lesson

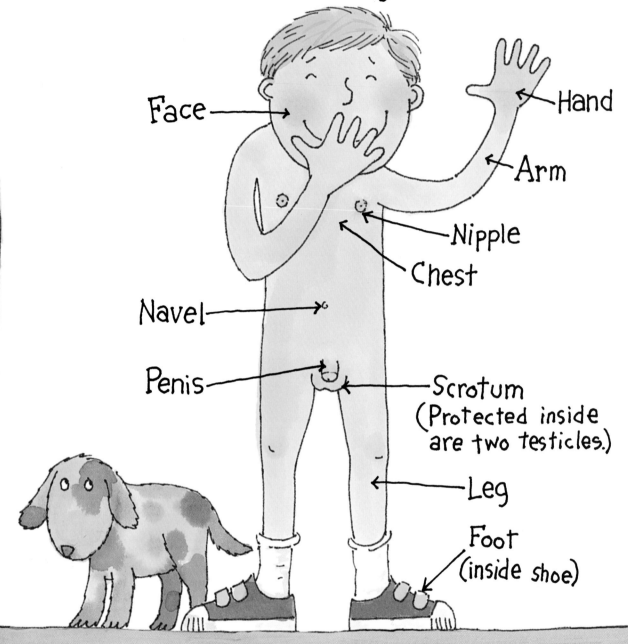

Face

Hand

Arm

Nipple

Chest

Navel

Penis

Scrotum
(Protected inside
are two testicles.)

Leg

Foot
(inside shoe)

Actually, the only sure way to tell boys and girls apart is by their *bodies*.

If you're a boy, you have a penis, scrotum, and testicles.

If you're a girl, you have a vulva, clitoris, and vagina.

These male and female body parts that show on the outside are called your genitals. Boys' genitals are easier to see than girls', but both are equally important.

Look! Our bodies are more alike than different!

Hand

Arm

Chest

Nipple

Navel

Vulva
(Protected inside are the clitoris and the opening to the vagina.)

Leg

Foot

Boys and girls also *use the toilet* differently.

A boy urinates through an opening in the tip of his penis. He can stand and aim his penis toward the toilet.

Peeing Demonstration
Not open to the public
Thank you.

A girl sits down and urinates through an opening inside her vulva called the urethra.

You may hear all kinds of words used to talk about girls' and boys' genitals. There are personal names, silly names, even rude, insulting names called swears. Some of us don't know what to call them!

Find out the correct names for as many parts of the body as you can.

Looking

It's natural to be interested in your own body and how it works. After all, nobody else in the world has a body exactly like yours. You're one of a kind. You're unique!

I'm going to draw myself, my whole body.

You may be curious about how other bodies look — other boys' or girls' or even your parents' — especially the parts usually covered up by clothes.

I'll show you mine.

Let's see.

Just remember that everyone's privacy needs to be respected . . . including yours!

Enjoying your body and the way it feels is an important part of being alive, no matter how old you are. Some parts of your body are more sensitive than others; do you feel more when you touch your elbow or your lips?

Touching and rubbing your genitals to feel good is called masturbation. Some of us try this; some of us don't. However, it's best to do this private kind of touching off by yourself.

Touching others is just as important. Whether it's hugging your parents, wrestling with a friend, or shaking your teacher's hand, touching brings you closer to someone.

Whoever you touch has feelings too. If someone doesn't want to be touched, then respect his or her wishes — don't do it!

Being Touched

From the moment a new baby is held and cuddled, she begins to learn how good it feels to be close to someone who loves her.

Everyone needs good touches to feel loved and happy. If you want a hug, you can say so.

But no one has the right to touch you in a way that feels wrong or uncomfortable.

If you don't like the way someone touches you, speak up and tell him or her to stop.

If that doesn't work, tell your mom or dad or another grown-up. Your body belongs to you, and you should say who touches it!

Why Boys and Girls Differ
A Little Lesson in Reproduction

All living things — plants, animals, and people — make other things that are just like them. Cats have kittens. Dogs have puppies. People have babies.

The sexual parts of girls and boys are made differently so that when they grow up they are able to create babies and become parents.

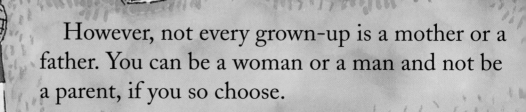

However, not every grown-up is a mother or a father. You can be a woman or a man and not be a parent, if you so choose.

Maybe later. I didn't know at your age. There must be a book about it.

ell your friends. You won't understand. You're too young.

Starting a Baby

It takes both a man and a woman to make a baby.

Inside a woman's body are tiny eggs, smaller than a dot. A man has even tinier sperm.

When a sperm combines with an egg, this now-fertilized egg is the beginning of a new baby! The change that takes place when a sperm enters an egg is called fertilization.

All boys and girls begin life this way. Imagine that!

Mom will know what to say.

My throat hurts.

I'm not ready.

embarrassing.

Dad, where do babies come from?

Umm. Uh, well, you see...I want to tell you, except...

21

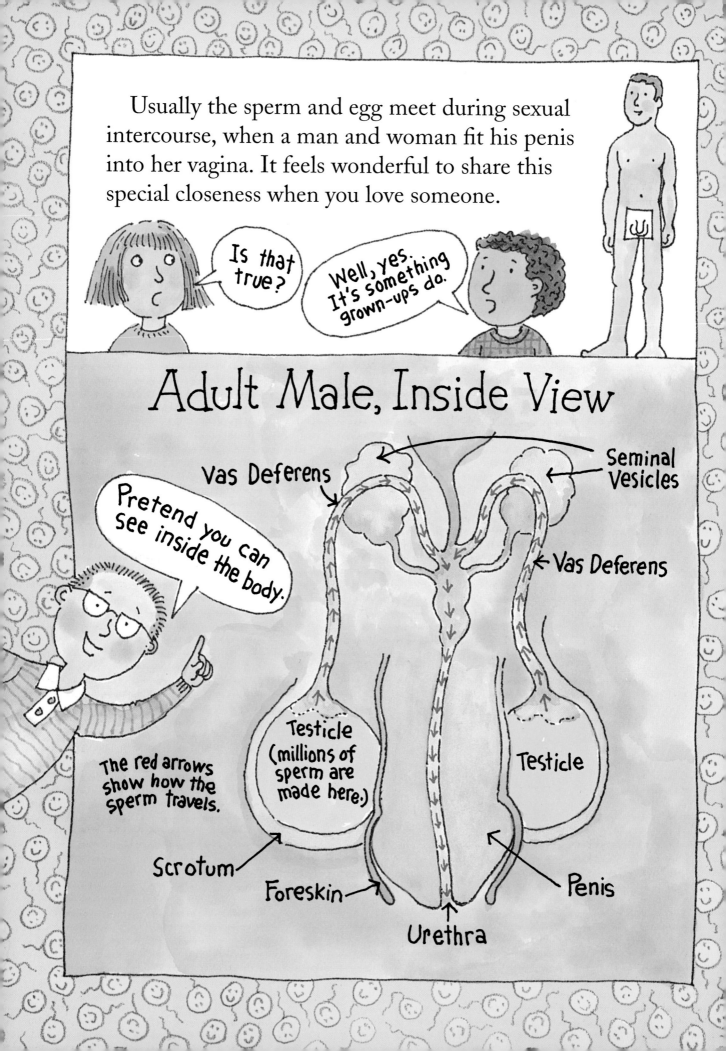

Inside the fertilized egg is information about how to shape this new life. These instructions, called genes, decide such things as a baby's skin color, the shape of its hands and feet, and its sex. Because genes come from both the father and mother, a child resembles each of its birth parents in some ways.

Adult Female, Inside View

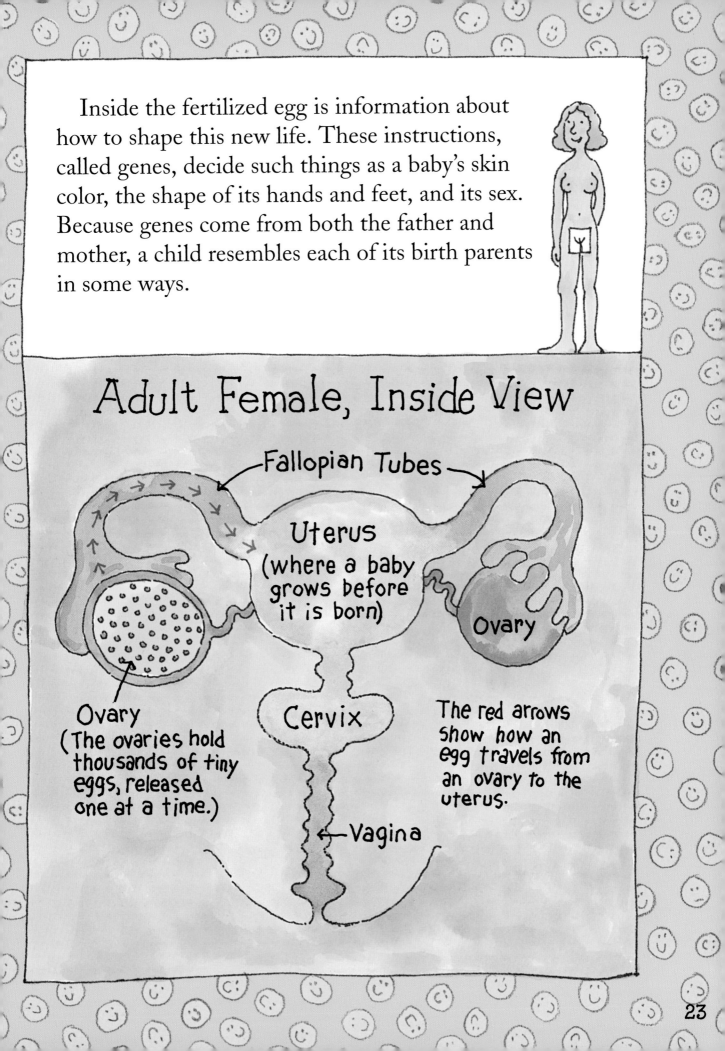

Fallopian Tubes

Uterus
(where a baby grows before it is born)

Ovary

Ovary
(The ovaries hold thousands of tiny eggs, released one at a time.)

Cervix

The red arrows show how an egg travels from an ovary to the uterus.

← Vagina

Growing a Baby

Very slowly, over several days, the fertilized egg travels into the mother's uterus, or womb. There it will grow and develop, first as a tiny embryo, then as a fetus who looks more and more like a baby.

The womb is a perfect first home: There the developing baby floats safe and protected inside a clear sac of warm liquid.

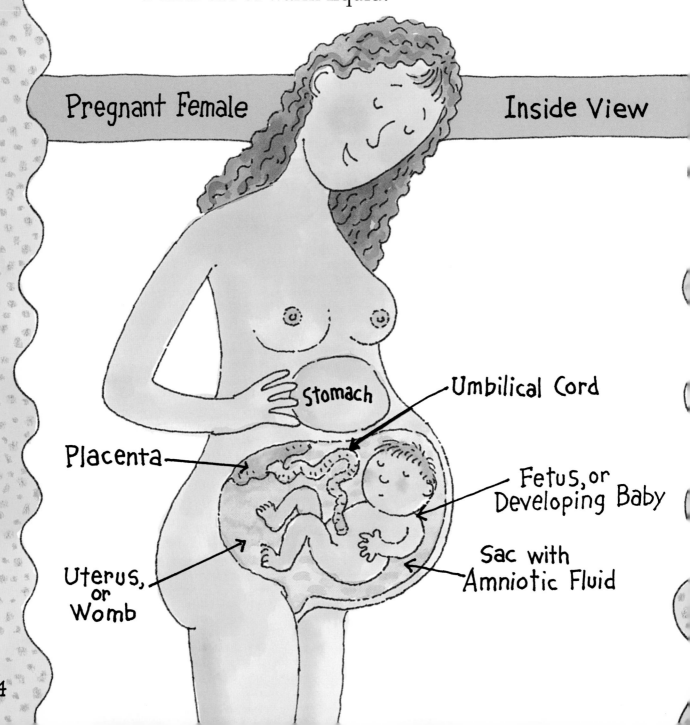

Pregnant Female   Inside View

Stomach

Umbilical Cord

Placenta

Fetus, or Developing Baby

Uterus, or Womb

Sac with Amniotic Fluid

Food and oxygen flow from the mother to the fetus through a flexible tube called the umbilical cord. Back through the cord travel the fetus's wastes, which are carried away by the mother's blood.

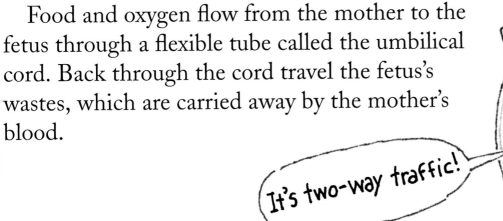

Awaiting a Baby

It takes a fetus about nine months to develop into a fully formed baby. When a mother has a baby growing inside her uterus, we say she is pregnant.

Having a Birth Day! (or Belly Button Day!)

When a baby is ready to be born, muscles in the mother's womb begin to tighten and relax, tighten and relax, helping her push out the baby. In most births, the baby comes out the vagina, which stretches to let it pass through.

Out comes the baby at last! The baby takes a first breath, her lungs open, and she lets out a cry! What an exciting, joyous event — the moment when a baby is born!

Once the umbilical cord is no longer needed, it can be cut. The place where it was attached becomes the navel, or belly button. Now the newborn baby is a separate person!

What Now?

From the moment your life begins, you are growing: on the outside, on the inside, in your own way, at your own speed.

When you're older, maybe ten or twelve or fourteen, your body gradually will change and your sex organs will develop. Going through these changes is called puberty.

But for today, enjoy being the girl or boy you are right now, with a body, mind, and spirit all your own!